Coach John and His Soccer Team

written by
ALICE K. FLANAGAN

photographs by
CHRISTINE OSINSKI

Reading Consultant
LINDA CORNWELL
Learning Resource Consultant
Indiana Department of Education

CHILDREN'S PRESS® _A Division of Grolier Publishing_
New York • London • Hong Kong • Sydney • Danbury, Connecticut

Special thanks to John Gurrieri
for allowing us to tell his story.

I would like to acknowledge my wife Elaine, who is the inspiration for everything I do, my beautiful daughter Sarah, who is the Lions unofficial assistant coach, and my son Johnny who plays every position, for the good of the team, without question.

I would also like to thank the soccer moms and dads who drop off, pick up, and cheer for us through rain, snow, wind, and cold. They are the true heroes. And of course all "Lions," past, present, and future. I will always hear their roar.

—John Gurrieri

Author's Note:
Coach John's last name is pronounced ga-RARE-ree.

Library of Congress Cataloging-in-Publication Data
Flanagan, Alice.
    Coach John and his soccer team / written by Alice K. Flanagan ; photographs by Christine Osinski.
        p. cm. — (Our neighborhood)
    Summary: Tells about a soccer coach who teaches his players to listen, get along with others, play hard, have fun, and be good sports even when they lose.
    ISBN 0-516-20777-6 (lib. bdg.)   0-516-26404-4 (pbk.)
    1. Soccer coaches—Juvenile literature. 2. Soccer—Juvenile literature. [1. Soccer.] I. Osinski, Christine, ill. II. Title. III. Series: Our neighborhood (New York, N.Y.)
GV943.25.F63 1998
796.334—dc21   97-45107
                                                                             CIP
                                                                             AC

Photographs ©: Christine Osinski

Listen to the people cheer!
A soccer game is about to begin.

Mr. Gurrieri coaches the Lions
soccer team in his spare time.
His players call him Coach John.

Ever since he was a boy, Coach John has liked playing sports.

When his son Johnny started school, Coach John started a soccer team and became its coach.

Coach John calls his team the Lions, because lions are quick, and lions have courage.

That's the way Coach John wants his team to play.

To get his team excited before every game, Coach John says, "Lions, let me hear you roar!"

Then he sends his team out
to play hard and have fun.

Coach John uses a whistle and a stopwatch during the game.

He keeps a first-aid kit and phone nearby in case someone gets hurt.

When Coach John was a boy, he usually wasn't picked first to be on a team. Sometimes, he didn't even get to play.

12

As a coach, he knows everyone on a team is important. He gives each of his players a chance to have fun.

While the players are having fun, Coach John is teaching them important things.

He teaches them to listen, to follow directions, to get along with others, and to play as a team.

Coach John shows them how to
follow the ball on the field and
control the ball with their feet.

He teaches them how to kick the
ball into the other team's net to
score a goal.

Each player has a job to do. It must be done in a special place on the field. Some players try to score goals.

Other players try to keep the other team from scoring.

A goalie stands in front of the net and tries to stop the ball from going in.

Only goalies can touch the ball with their hands.

Time out! The team needs a break.

On the side-lines, Coach John's wife and daughter are watching to see if something's wrong.

But the players just need a drink.
And Coach John has something
to tell his team.

He says, "Stay in your places on the field. Keep your heads up and follow the ball. Even when you'd like to stop, keep on going and don't give up."

Soon the game is over. The Lions
lost. But the players are not upset.

They thank the other team for playing. The Lions are good sports.

Coach John is proud of his team. The Lions know how to play hard and have fun.

29

The team is proud of Coach John, too.
He's a coach who loves his players.
He's a coach who loves what he does.

Meet the Author
and the Photographer

Alice Flanagan and Christine Osinski are sisters.
They grew up together telling stories and drawing
pictures in a brown brick bungalow in a southwest-
side neighborhood of Chicago, Illinois. Today they
write stories and take photographs professionally.

Ms. Flanagan resides in Chicago with her husband
and works as a freelance writer. Ms. Osinski is a
photographer and teaches at The Cooper Union for
the Advancement of Science and Art in New York
City. She lives with her husband and two sons in
Ridgefield, Connecticut.